anythink

What's an Election?

Nancy Kelly Allen

Educational Media

rourkeeducationalmedia.com

www.rourkeeducationalmedia.com

PHOTO CREDITS: Cover: © Diana Walters, © WendellandCarolyn; Title Page: © nicolesy, akkul; Page 3: © laflor; Page 4: © 3d_kot; Page 5: © JBryson; Page 6: © Carsten Reisinger; Page 7: Kevin Carden ©; Page 9: © Michael Flippo; Page 11: © ; Gary Hathaway; Page 13: © inhauscreative; Page 14: © LivingImages, Skypixel; Page 15: © selimaksan; Page 17: © plherrera; Page 18: © lisafx, YinYang; Page 19: © DougSchneiderPhoto, Jose Gil; Page 20: © asiseeit; Page 21: © JodiJacobson; Page 22: © GYI NSEA, WendellandCarolyn, Michael Flippo, Sven Klaschik; Page 23: © KentWeakley, Gary Hathaway, YinYang

Edited by Precious McKenzie
Cover design by Tara Raymo
Interior design by Cory Davis

Library of Congress Cataloging-in-Publication Data

What's an Election? / Nancy Kelly Allen
(Little World Social Studies)
ISBN 978-1-61810-144-0 (hard cover) (alk. paper)
ISBN 978-1-61810-277-5 (soft cover)
Library of Congress Control Number: 2011945871

Rourke Educational Media
Printed in the United States of America,
North Mankato, Minnesota

rourkeeducationalmedia.com

customerservice@rourkeeducationalmeida.com • PO Box 643328 Vero Beach, Florida 32964

Today is **Election** Day. An election is a decision made by voting.

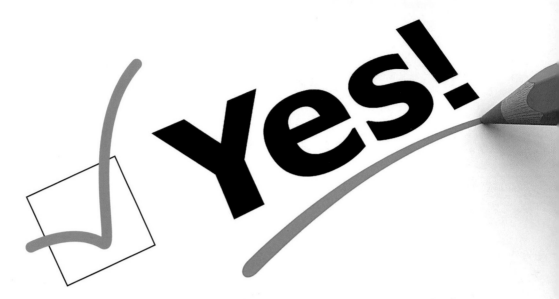

An election is a way people can make their **opinions** count.

We may **vote** with friends to choose which game to play, tag or jump rope?

On Election Day, adults vote
for leaders, such as senators and
a president.

National Election Day in the United States is the Tuesday following the first Monday in November. Other elections are held at different times.

An election begins when people say they are running for **office**, which means they are trying to get a special job, or duty, in public service.

Before becoming president, Barack Obama was the
Democratic candidate.

In the United States, **candidates** who run for office belong to a political party.

The two main political parties are Democrat and Republican.
Their symbols are the donkey and the elephant.

11

Candidates make speeches and tell the people what they will do as their leaders. As their leaders, their job is to serve the public.

Candidates promise to work to make people's lives better. Some promise to make new laws or change old laws.

All United States citizens who are at least 18 years old have the right to vote.

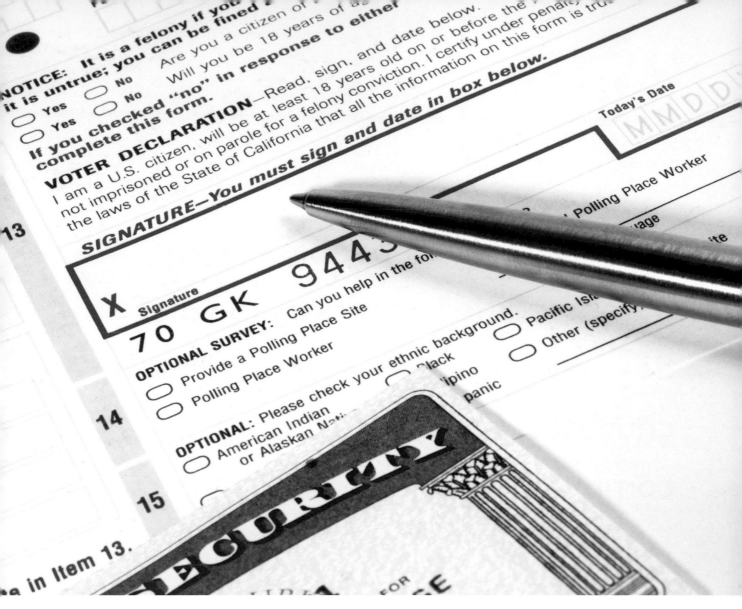

When you turn 18 you must register to vote. When you register you choose if you want to be a Republican, a Democrat, or an Independent.

On Election Day people line up at many different places to vote. Sometimes people vote in schools, churches, firehouses, or community centers.

The place where people vote is called the polls.

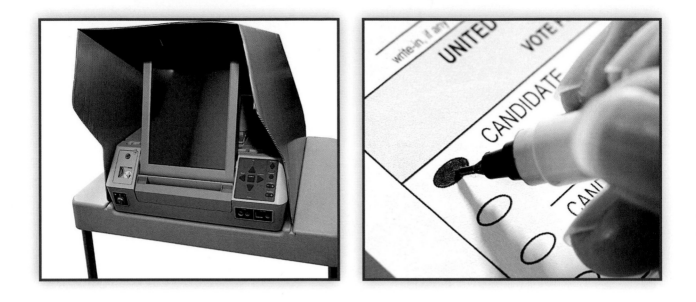

Some voters use machines and some vote on paper **ballots**. The candidate with the most votes wins.

In the United States, all election votes are secret.

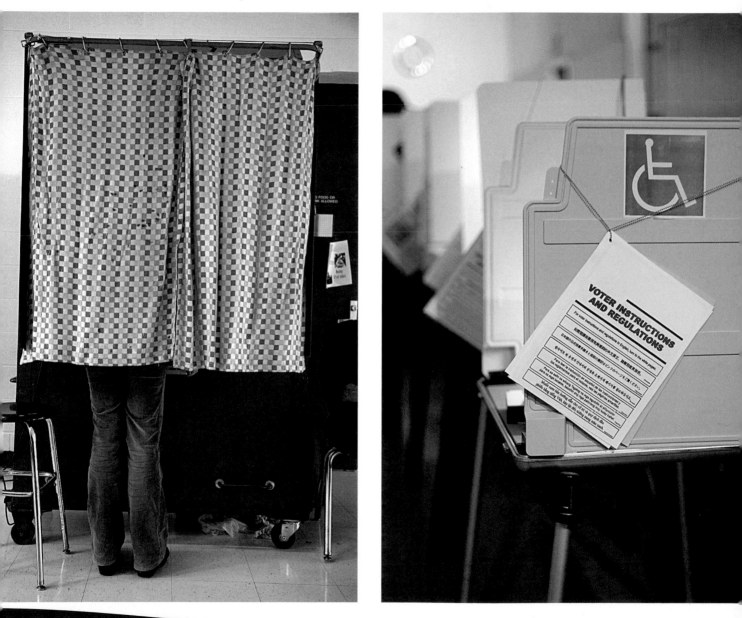

Some people consider the right to vote to be the most important right Americans have.

Picture Glossary

ballots (BAL-uhts): Ballots are sheets of paper used for secret voting.

candidates (KAN-di-deytss): Candidates are people who seek an office in an election.

election (ih-LEK-shuhn): Election is a decision made by voting.

office (AH-fes): An office is a special job or duty.

opinions (uh-PIN-yuhns): Opinions are beliefs people have.

vote (VOHT): To vote means to make a choice in an election.

Index

ballots   18

candidate(s)   9, 10, 12, 13, 18

Democrat   11, 15

election(s)   3, 4, 6, 7, 8, 16, 19

office   8, 10

political party(ies)   10, 11

polls   17, 20

Republican   11, 15

vote(s)   5, 6, 14-21

Websites

pbskids.org/democracy/vote

www.congressforkids.net/Elections_electionday.htm

www.apples4theteacher.com/holidays/election-day

About the Author

Nancy Kelly Allen ran for class president when she was a young girl in school in Kentucky. After the votes were cast and the ballots were counted, she won! Nancy thanked everyone who voted for her in the election.

Ask The Author!
www.rem4students.com